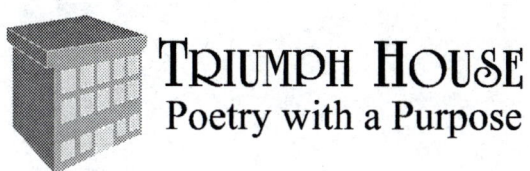

MIRRORED EMOTIONS

Edited by

CHRIS WALTON

To Pam
Many Thanx for a
great evening Tom
See Page 5   xx

First published in Great Britain in 1998 by
TRIUMPH HOUSE
1-2 Wainman Road, Woodston,
Peterborough, PE2 7BU
Telephone (01733) 230749

All Rights Reserved

Copyright Contributors 1998

HB ISBN 1 86161 203 6
SB ISBN 1 86161 208 7

FOREWORD

Mirrored Emotions is a unique collection of poems by over 100 new and established authors.

Each of the poets included in this special anthology, use their creativity to offer their stories, memories and messages to others as they write about the many important elements that make and mould our lives.

The book takes you on a journey where you experience all aspects of life, from fantasy to reality. *Mirrored Emotions* gives the reader a unique insight into the many different facets of people's lives whilst revealing their innermost thoughts and feelings.

Contained within this book you will find many different styles of poetry; from traditional to contemporary, but whatever the theme or style you can still be assured of a truly entertaining and enjoyable read.

Chris Walton
Editor

CONTENTS

Pattern Of The Day	Alec Williams	1
An Englishman's Home	S C Wiggins	2
Go Back To Your Wife	Top Cat	3
A Face	Irene Grant	4
It's Worth The Wait	M Rossi	5
Passion Sunday	Joan Woolard	6
The Row	Janet Brown	7
Recalling June 1997	Florence Andrews	8
Forsythia	Bob Bedwell	9
Exam Room	Michael C Foster	10
A Warning	Junor T Baker	11
Harvest Home	A J Don	12
Yesteryear	Roslyn	13
The Kiss	J M H Barton	14
France, Here We Come!	Sarah Evans	15
Our Garden In Spring	Norman Mason	16
The Stream	C Watson	17
The Lollipop Lady	David Sheasby	18
Waves Of Love	Fay Evans	19
St Albans' Grand Steeplechase	T M Tapping	20
Panic Of The Titanic	Karen Henderson	21
Summer In Full Dress . . .	Irene Spencer	22
'Owed' To Millions . . .	Inga Dean	24
Broken Hearted In Concrete City	Kevin Herbert	25
Raindrops On The Window	Ian Liddle	26
The Cosmic Poet	Edward Graham Macfarlane	27
My Shadow	Jennifer C Kerr	28
To London	Francis 'Gunner' Hodges	29
A Winter Rhyme	Thomas George	30
Unsung Heroes	GIG	31
Lest We Forget	Judy Studd	32
Changes	Jacqueline Richmond Jones	34
Empty	Robert D Shooter	35
Memories	Carla Jones	36
October Bride	Ken Lowe	37

Computers!	Sheri Dean	38
Flower In Bloom	Dorothy Conway Trilk	39
Never	J S Elliott	40
Our Princess Diana	Ivy Blades	41
Full Stop	Stephan Wegner	42
Reflections	A J De-Arden	43
Love Story	Vera Fertash	44
Grapes On The Vine	Maria Gallo	45
Locked Inside	Jan Nice	46
I Love Scotland	Helen Manson	47
To Forgive Is Divine	Kathryn Morgan	48
Pictures From Words	Janet Allen	49
My Life	Claire Haughin	50
Ha! Ha! Ha!	Lynn Harper	51
The Road Of Life	Terry White	52
The Silence Of The Night	Nathalie El-Korashy	53
Prayer	Vera Porter	54
Vampire	Caz Rioche	55
The Child	Catherine Whittaker	56
It's Only A Game	Aline McInnes Ross	57
The Midnight Stallion	Shaun Gilbertson	58
Someone Special	Brenda Baker	59
My Lady	Frank Richards	60
Millennium Resolutions	Carolyn Coyne	61
Sleepy Dartmoor	Pat Heppel	62
Classic Gold We Love You	Coleen Bradshaw	63
Forever (Life Must Go On)	Bakewell Burt	64
Through A Glass, Brightly	David Tallach	65
Garden Of Eden	Lea Rochelle	66
Today	J Palmer	67
Your Picture	Keith Farley	68
For The Love Of One Son - Gentle Giant	Susan Goldsmith	69
Feeling Safe	Jean Calver	70
Those Lazy Days Of Summer	Violet Bainbridge	71
Forever Hopeful	Mia Ryan	72
Future	R A Sangster	74
Cosy	Gail Susan Halstead	75

My Day At The Races	D W Andrews	76
Donald's Day	Sylvia E Armer	77
Win Some, Lose Some	Doreen Priestley	78
On The Beach	A P Dixson	80
Disused Airfield	Jessica Frank	81
A Writer's Commision	Julie McKenzie	82
True Friend	Edna Ball	83
Final Journey Of A Passenger Liner	Diana Griffiths	84
Outside Of Basingstoke	Margaret E Gaines	85
Listen To Us Our Rights	Velma Winstanley	86
Stillness	Dave Mountjoy	87
Neon Angels	Carole House	88
Life Can Be Sweet	P A Deakin	89
A Career in IT	Suzanne Fowler	90
August '96	Samuel Down	91
God's Rainbow	Barbara Quimby	92
I Saw A Butterfly	Karen Monaghan	93
Memories	Owen Edwards	94
Trusting People	Danielle Turner	95
The Alcoholic	Claire Partridge	96
Dream Children	P McNeil	97
The Coppered Dream	Kim Montia	98
Walk With Me	Paul Willis	99
Footprints In The Snow	Patricia Whittle	100
Remembering Me	Ivan J Peck	102
Share A Forest	Des Lamb	103
One To One Hundred	Marion Elvera	104
Just Perfect	E Jones	105
Pessimist And Optimist	Sonia Coneye	106
My Pledge Of Honour	Simon King	107
A Mum	Sian Sparks	108
Digging Holes	John Dobson	109
Tales From The Riverbank	John Palmer	110
Another World	Teresa Smith	111
Waiting	Patricia Wardle	112
Trouble	T Burke	113
Why Worry	Brian Marshall	114

I Love You More Everyday	Terry Collins	115
If Only Life Was A Ball Of Wool	Veronica Black	116
Apart No More	Alan Jones	117
I Am You	Tracy Mitchell	118

PATTERN OF THE DAY

I have the pattern of the day,
it's not like bottled Oil Ulay.
Neither is it tinned or wrapped,
or like a pet caged or trapped,
or muses round without no say.

Not small but large and in most ways,
around it gathers when honest man prays.
And never to be overlapped,
the pattern of the day.

Scarlet brings it out to play,
it hurries now without delay.
Attracting many who have mapped,
that which falls on man uncapped.
And I for one will hold it's tray,
the pattern of the day.

Alec Williams

An Englishman's Home

An Englishman's home is his castle, is a saying one often hears said
when in fact that Englishman's castle, may be little more than a shed
for it's a question of pride in one's castle, not necessarily the size
which when said to some people, will bring a great look of surprise
to the average man it means status, the place in which he lives
so the bigger the house he lives in, to him the more pleasure it gives
but some of us look at it quite different, it's comfort not
                                        size that we like
when going from one room to another, we don't want to get on a bike
but then of course in we English, there are those that some call a snob
who turn their nose at the dustman, just because of his job
but then he too has his castle, which will always be home to him
and if he did not come out of his castle, who then would empty their bin
I do not look down on my dustman, though sometimes I do get irate
I don't object to him leaving the drawbridge, if only he'd just
                                                        shut the gate.

S C Wiggins

GO BACK TO YOUR WIFE

Go on; go back to your wife,
Me; I'm just your lover,
I'm the one you put on a pedestal,
Then had to run for cover,
I'm the one that sits and 'cries'
In my empty vacant house
Trying to pick up my life.
Go on; go now; go back to your wife.

Top Cat

A Face

The face at the window
Seemed to be watching
As I prepared to leave the room
With lights ablaze, in the early evening,
If full view without the curtains!
How long were you there?
At a distance
I puzzled, who could it be,
Till remembered empathy, cured me,
Perhaps, of the suspicion,
That you were planted,
In my line of vision!

Irene Grant

IT'S WORTH THE WAIT

Be still my fickle heart, don't
play games with me.
My mind's the real joker, and this is
not to be.
Be patient and wait for the real love.
The real love to come along.
It's not enough to desire love.
You must feel love,
and be strong.
I will wait my love for
you to come along.

M Rossi

PASSION SUNDAY

Two squashed frogs lay on the lane,
Bonded together as one,
Forever joined in death's last pain,
United on life's last run.

Caught unawares, 'love is blind',
The couple's troth was plighted
In passionate haste to be entwined
These lovers were unsighted.

So when you face the storms of love
With your hatches left unbattened,
Remember the sad tale above
Of frogs *in flagrante* flattened.

Joan Woolard

THE ROW

He's turned his back on me again,
So he's sulking another night.
Why can't he just apologise
When he knows I'm always right.
He's only pretending to be asleep,
Sometimes I do hate men,
If he'd only try to talk to me
I could snub him once again.
How dare he think of going to sleep
When he knows he made me cry.
Well, I wasn't really crying
But I thought it worth a try.
And when I said I was leaving
He even offered to pack my case,
He really did enjoy that
I could tell by the smirk on his face.
Just wait until tomorrow
He'll get beans on toast for his tea,
And I'll have another migraine.
That'll teach him to upset me.

Janet Brown

RECALLING JUNE 1997

Father whatever are
Your angels thinking,
Loving kindness to flowers
I understand very well,
But even they must believe
This kind comes from hell.

I have to stand by and see
My beautiful flowers blooming in mud,
We are no longer visited by bees,
I have a suggestion, make one plea
Perhaps you should
Look, take pity on flowers and me.

The skies must be nearly dry,
Is the sun still up there?
My garden is enough to make one cry,
Talk of blossoms in the dust,
I tried so hard but suppose I must
Start all over again - in the rain!

Florence Andrews

FORSYTHIA

Golden bells in gardens
suddenly appear
heralding a brand new spring
Forsythia is here

four wee petals on a stem
make a thousand fold
little chunks of sunshine them
goodbye winter cold.

Bob Bedwell

EXAM ROOM

Heads bent, a common urgency prevails,
And tension hangs oppressive in the hall.
Some confidently write, but many pause,
Eyes glazed or fixed on distant memory.
An anxious frown gives way to blank despair.
Two years of work condense within the span
Of three short hours; all futures are at stake.
Too many wasted days betray a few,
Their minds beleaguered, undernourished, dry.
A frantic scribbling as the minutes drain.
Some sit resigned; but some, self-satisfied,
Check watches, finish off, sit back and smile.
Time's up. Stop writing. Headings, names, Admin.
Release: and sudden, loud, excited chat
Recedes and leaves a blank, a bathos here,
A flatness. Then the packing up of scripts . . .

Michael C Foster

A Warning

Driving back one evening through the deserted Yorkshire moors
When the birds were all drowsy with sleep
I felt very alone and forgotten
I stopped, for one moment I jerked alive

Something had passed through me
That altered and enlightened my brain
A bleak and uncoded message
Whispered down all my nerves
Leave this place
You are alone
My nerves tensed up
I felt as if I was glued to my seat
My fingers felt numb
And I found it difficult to turn the ignition key in my car
Eventually I drove away
But it left me feeling very uneasy

Something in the wind smelt of death
There was great mystery and gloom
Driving along I noticed the long lean curves
And the melancholy moor

Thinking back on that day
Something or someone had passed
A finger through my abstract reasoning
Was it my imagination
Or was it something else?

Junor T Baker

HARVEST HOME

The rowdy cawing of the crow
Resounds in summer sun
'Cross rippling fields of golden corn
Where harvest has begun;

Too soon a frightened field mouse runs
To find a new terrain
And leaves the ever hungry birds
To steal the yellow grain;

And there the panting collie dog
Amongst the cornflow'r mops
Is chasing bees and butterflies
Whilst toilers gather crops;

And when the heavy load is stacked
And nature's free to roam
The silent ev'ning shadows creep
Upon the harvest home.

A J Don

YESTERYEAR

My mind goes back to yesteryear
When I was young and slim
But now I'm old and grey
Being more fat than thin
But I've memories of days gone by
I've time now to sit and sigh
Pictures come and go
Of people that I used to know
Seem to be waiting to bring to mind
Things I have done and left undone.

Roslyn

THE KISS

Unexpected was your kiss that summer's night,
With pain, sadness, silent rivers bright;
Shaking, tremulous, heart in systole's grasp
Lightening, the world crashed as shattered glass.

Love was calling, love called that night,
Awakening emotions, crashing oceans might;
Without birth, died Bacchanalian madness.
No drug more potent than beauty's sadness.

Eyes pure of beauteous love pervade
Without linger, but the briefest masquerade;
Carmined those lips, unknown such hunger sought
In measureless captivity, tenderness caught.

Dramatic a friendship, when love incline,
Powerful, heady, rich perfumed wine;
Silent enchantment love's beauty love's plight,
Life immortal love's vision, that summer's night.

J M H Barton

FRANCE, HERE WE COME!

We had Euro '96, now we come to conquer the world!
Football's what we do, we sure know how to play,
With Shearer up front, what more can I say.
Super kid Michael, will surely play his part too,
When it comes to scoring, he knows what to do!

Then there's McManaman dodging every defender in sight,
He'll give it a go, he's in for the fight.
But still, we need that little bit of flare,
I look around and Redknapp's there.

When it comes to defence, we're very lucky too,
We've got Batty and Campbell, they know what to do.
In David Seaman, we've got a great keeper,
He's so skilled, we don't need to look deeper.

Remember, France here we come,
We'll be there with the band and drums.
To honour England and our football too,
We're three lions, through and through.

Sarah Evans (14)

Our Garden In Spring

The daffodils now in full bloom
waving in the gentle breeze, saying
'Please take notice of me, I am
the most prominent of all spring flowers.'

The primroses and other flowers,
being of lesser breed than the daffs
all have a message of spring to give.

The squirrel now almost out from
hibernation, now spring is here
scampers up the tree in high delight.
Other birds and animals enjoy this season too.

The goldfish in the garden pond are
now making an appearance, waiting
for food scattered on the water.

Also not forgetting the budding of
shrubs, trees and plants, all getting
ready for high summer.

Oh my! The lawn needs mowing, not a
job for older people of tender age.

The deck and garden chairs all need
an airing to catch the sunshine
when it appears to shine.

Norman Mason

THE STREAM

Fine, bold curves,
Gleefully dart and twist,
Pursuing their spiralling friends.
Like playful youngsters,
Exploring their watery world.

Streaks flail and fold,
As swaying anemones that cower and close.
Irregular ovals elongate,
Like screaming deformed faces.
Writhing ripples merge in conflict,
A boisterous struggle for their existence.

Roaring surges of water,
Plunging fearlessly down
Into eerie depths below.
Translucent curtains,
Shimmering in the radiant sun.

The deep tranquil pool
A glazed, mottled surface,
Still and silent.
As a sleeping being
Aged with time.

C Watson

THE LOLLIPOP LADY

There once was a lollipop lady
Helping children to cross the road
Some walked quite nice and behaved themselves
But others acted like toads.

On sunny mornings
Some mothers stop by for a chat
Some tell of all their troubles
And the men talk of this and that.

Some holidays are long ones
And some mothers think that they are a pain
But when at last they are all over
There are tears because it is all back to school again.

Wet days are a problem,
Standing in the rain
All she can dream of is home
And watch the water running down the drains.

But when the day is over
And she puts her stick away
All she really wants to do
Is say Hip, Hip, Hooray!

David Sheasby

WAVES OF LOVE

The waves were crashing against
the rocks with a raging force.

The sky was evil looking

And the clouds were moving in fast
and fiercely.

But I wasn't afraid

I was in my man's arms, full of warmth,
and the only rage here, was love.

Fay Evans

ST ALBANS' GRAND STEEPLECHASE

I've got six prints on the wall
Of the steeplechase to beat them all
Over the fences, six feet tall
They thundered along one and all
Riders fell at every fence
And all for the sake of a few pence
Horses snorting in the cold air
Riders warm with the rum punch
All ready for the crunch,
Over hill and over dale
They ran like the wind that day
Moonraker won by half a length
Four miles he ran to win the prize
A gallant horse and others beside.

J M Tapping

Panic Of The Titanic

Calm as sea can be
no worries, no hurry
'Unsinkable' was the cry.
Panic unfolds, lifesavers issued
hope has gone, last boat afloat
no room left
moan, music and screams
Prayers being said, forgiveness craved,
dying sounds all around.
Down it goes, slowly
to the icy black bottom.
Bodies bobbing, frozen solid
babes, women, men huddled together.
Forever asleep two miles down.
Those who lived the horror,
survivors, they're called,
retell the tale
of a few days in April
when a ship set sail
and all the heartache it brought.

Karen Henderson

SUMMER IN FULL DRESS . . .

Throughout the world there is beauty
Breathtaking . . . awesome and fair
Waterfalls, deserts, mountain peaks.
Forests with plants so rare
But here on this little island
When summer is in, full dress
If you look . . . take time out to look
There is beauty only we possess
The beautiful greens of summer
Trees of every hue
Rolling hills and lowlands
Basking beneath skies of blue
Meadows . . . the grass growing tall now
Moving lazily in the breeze
But as you pass by idly
They look like rolling seas
Lanes banked high on either side
Take a look and see
For there are hundreds of wild flowers
Growing together in harmony
And as you turn a corner
You get a pleasant surprise
You see a scene so lovely
It brings tears to your eyes
Cottages nestling together
With roses round the door
Each one decked out in full summer dress
Cottage gardens with flowers galore
And standing like a sentinel
A church in subtle stone
Guarding this quiet and tranquil scene
Where beauty reigns alone

So as you jet off to exotic lands
However far you roam
Remember, with summer in full dress
The beauty you've left at home . . .

Irene Spencer

'OWED' TO MILLIONS...

Who will dig them a brand new well?
Who will help them to buy and sell?
Millions of faces going through hell -
Who cares?

Some do, some don't.
Who will help?
Some will, some won't

Millions of *people,* facing the day,
Thousands upon thousands without a say;
Hundreds and hundreds with next to no pay -
Who cares?

Some do, some don't.
And *who* will help?
some will, some won't...

Think of the *souls* you are casting aside:
Sisters and brothers taken for a ride;
Thousands of children with nowhere to hide -
Who cares?

Some do, some don't.
And who will help?
Some will, some won't.

Meaningless horrors take place *every day;*
Dribbles and morsels their only stay -
What shall they do tomorrow - today?
But who *cares?*

Some do, some don't
And who will help?
Some will, some won't...

Inga Dean

BROKEN HEARTED IN CONCRETE CITY

Rain washed streets, street
lamps cast a yellow glow, down
came the rain bouncing off the
concrete, no hungry earth to
drink it in, repelled by slabs of
concrete.

How can we know the hardness of
concrete city when our hearts are
just the same.

Awesome neon signs light up the
whole night and street, sending
coloured messages into her brain.

She couldn't comprehend how the
tramp in the shop doorway could
make that place his home, he knows
the stark reality of concrete city.

Taxi cabs prowl the streets. The
all night bar staff have to face
the morning, and then sleep to
face the next harrowing night.

She stooped down and picked up
someone's love letter lying in
the gutter, dying words etched on
paper by a wounded heart, he
failed to get into her heart, the
girl from concrete city left him
broken hearted.

Kevin J Herbert

RAINDROPS ON THE WINDOW

Raindrops on the window
People splash by
Oblivious
To the watcher
As he tries in vain
To analyse
Life's every bane.

Hurtling past
Goes another crammed train
Hundreds of hearts
Holding mixed happiness and pain.

Millions of thoughts
Rushing through everyone's brain
Trying to cope
Or trying to evade
Ultimately demanding
Crushing emotions of love and pain.

Keeping head afloat
Staying sane
Stuck in the fast lane
No chance to slow
Catch a breath.

Watching
Thinking
What?
Raindrops on the window.

Ian Liddle

THE COSMIC POET

Some say the entire universe,
Was made by one great God
But cosmic poets don't accept this,
Say it is scientifically odd.

The cosmic poetry of science,
Is therefore clearly seen,
To be truer than all former folk
Have thought about our cosmic scene.

The very latest gadgets,
Are all around them when,
They need warmth or sustenance,
Within a scientific regimen.

The business of such poets,
Is new gadgets to conceive,
To improve the people welfare,
Whilst they all live and breathe.

Edward Graham Macfarlane

My Shadow

My shadow watches me,
following from behind,
always in pace with me,
never out of time.

My shadow is my keeper
an angel of some kind
Sent to watch from heaven,
even in the darkest times.

My shadow is a mirror of me,
but different in its way
It never leaves me lonely
but, cowardly, hides away.

My shadow is still a stranger
but if that mirror breaks,
we will meet together
and slowly fade away.

Jennifer C Kerr

TO LONDON

They stood their ground, when none knew what.
The next night or day would be their lot.
And in the years to come, let's not forget,
Those stout hearts of London best.

For they live on through Hitler's hate,
Caring not was their fate.
But waited for a golden dawn,
Good luck, God bless you, London born.

Francis 'Gunner' Hodges (Deceased)

A Winter Rhyme

A touch of snow,
Cold winds blow,
Iced up cars,
Dewy grass.

Winter has arrived.

Bare trees,
Cold knees,
People sneeze,
People freeze.

Winter has arrived.

Children love to go out to play,
Others don't like the weather today,
Adults think it's bitterly cold,
They say 'We'll stay in, we're getting too old.'

Winter has arrived.

Thomas George (10)

UNSUNG HEROES

Names are written on marbled stone
Faceless heroes who gave their best
Scarlet poppies adorn green fields
Where so many laid to rest.

Front line people, young and old
So proud to play their part
Fighting for a way of life
In a war they didn't start.

Battle weary, mentally scarred
They marched into oblivion
Honours won, with battle lost
Someone's child, every one of them.

Time may fade most memories
But we must never forget those who
Marched away to fight a cause
And gave their lives for me and you.

Their eyes shall never see again
The joy that freedom is
But we salute them one and all
Who perished so we could live . . .

GIG

LEST WE FORGET

The Cenotaph Memorial rose piercingly grey
Old soldiers' medals shone in the broad light of day
Remembering the years when in unison they'd marched
Plus the dirt, dust and blisters; their mouths that were parched

With wrinkled faces which were once etched in pain
They remembered their comrades who had all been slain
The bright firework display held the eve before
Seemed so frivolous now in the light of a war

The Queen stood so sombre in bright autumn light
Whilst the three major parties and Commonwealth unite
But the air hung heavy as light rain still fell
Prince Philip laid a wreath but he didn't look well

Red poppies in wreaths around the Cenotaph lay
War heroes recalled with glazed eyes like a play
I watched it on screen; felt detached from it all
For some it was two great world wars they recall

For in memories mists of times that won't heal
No words can describe how these war veterans feel
As each paid tribute and remembered their friends
Plus the sleepless nights and the days without end . . .

Our freedom was fought; the world wars had been won
Friendships were forged in a scorched desert sun
Great Britain fell silent as Big Ben chimed
But the rain streamed heavier and very well timed

I remember another great war that was won
Not fought by battalions but Jesus, God's son
The world was in darkness when He died for our sin
The devil lay cowering for he knew who would win

And we don't have to fight on our own any more
For the battle is His as like eagles we soar
Jesus has triumphed o'er sin, death and hell
And the father of lies who from heaven once fell.

These battles we fight on this earth may be tough
But a day will soon dawn when He'll say 'That's enough!'
Let's hasten that day when he comes as a King
And the Cenotaph Memorial won't mean a thing.

Judy Studd

CHANGES

Away slipped the veil, off Myfanwy's face, still pale
as the sunlight warmed her skin.
She opened her eyes,
looked up at the skies.
It felt good, to wake once again.
She looked around the room, now empty and bare.
No coal on the fire, and mam's not there.
So she walked through the door,
down the old road once more
To play with her friend once again.

There were no games to be played
because there's a penny arcade,
where the lush green fields used to be.
Vile words from the young,
chewing their gum,
they seem to have lost all their dignity.
Turning away, her eyes opened wide,
she could not stop staring at the greatness in size
of the grey iron towers that belched from the ground
where the oaks grew thick, now a tree can't be found.

A factory stood where the flowers had been.
No buttercups, daisies or rambling roses are seen.
Even the crocus would grow in the snow,
but now there's no room for the flowers to grow.
She walked up the hill, and through the door
her little wet feet left marks on the floor.
She lay on the couch and gave a long sigh,
with a smile on her face, she closed her eyes.
There is no noise to be heard and nothing to say.
Because there's nothing left for Myfawnwy, down our way.

Jacqueline Richmond Jones

EMPTY
(In fond memory of Mutti and Ray)

Silence seemed insistent - unbearable -
the flurry of letters storing stable
emptiness - annihilation of home.
Unusual smell of stale air does come
dispelling spirit of place - enable

motivation to open window - pull
fresh air through house. Radio is able
to still the heavy nothing which comes from
silence.

Much of the furniture has gone too. Cull
of house whilst jungle of garden growth. Bull
needed to clear wild grass, bulging growth. Come
back to life! Collect takeaway - bring home
to eat - isolation - vulnerable.
Silence.

Robert D Shooter

MEMORIES

I still remember that special place
where we both loved to go

Down beneath the wooden bridge
where that river used to flow

For me my fondest memories
are captured inside my heart

The time we kissed and cuddled
and never wished to part.

Your gentle kiss so precious
your touch so soft and sweet

You were never sad or quiet
but sometimes quite discreet

The image of you so special
almost as vivid as today

The dancing along the riverbank
and those games we used to play.

The hours we spent together
were filled with passion and devotion

You were everything I wanted
and for you I showed emotion

As the memory I have is fading
I feel my whole world is evading.

But those times have been and gone
now and these thoughts are still within

So I will carry on as normal and let
my new life begin.

Carla Jones

OCTOBER BRIDE

I see you as a rose,
You are like the bud of early spring.
Tightly clad, desperate to free those limbs,
As you await summer warmth.

For I alone know of those red petals
Impatient to burst,
To bloom,
More lovely and longer,
Than those October roses
Ever close to your heart.

Ken Lowe

COMPUTERS!

Once again I am here, this mouse in my hand,
Trying to use a computer, that I hardly understand.
I try to ask a question, from the wizard who's so wise,
But all he seems to do, is to smile and roll his eyes.
No doubt as time goes on, I shall learn just what to do,
But as a body ages, the brain lets things fall through!
So instead of information logging on where it should be,
I seem to just remember what I have to cook for tea.
Perhaps I should give up the fight, and simply rest at ease,
Forget about this learning, which really is a tease.
But then I never did do, the things I should have done,
I'm sure that if I had, life wouldn't be such fun!
I'll never grow old gracefully; conform as they say,
So I'll be here again tomorrow, just like I was today.

Sheri Dean

FLOWER IN BLOOM

Young girl awakening
Spirit as free as the air
With no worries or cares
Floating with the leaves in the breeze
All your dreams of yesterday.
Welcoming the spring with open arms.
As your beauty bursts open like the buds in the earth
Exploding like the sunrise on a human face.
Growing lovelier every day
Unrestricted in this, your time.
Mixed with the showers, and the sun.
The tears and laughter, for summer fun.
At this time, no thought appears,
Of autumn, and then winter comes.
Enjoy your liberty while you may.
For nothing will ever be quite the same.

Dorothy Conway Trilk

NEVER

Her voice did not say much,
but from her eyes;
from her eyes
came the thoughts of a million years,
tumbling through time
on an endless quest for a being
in which to lay to rest,
for want of a moment's sleep.
And never a word was said.
Yet emotions leapt and cried
to the fortunate looker
upon those eyes,
and spelled a dream,
moment, by moment, by glorious moment;
And spelled a wish
And spelled a scene
And spelled a love -

And never a word was said.

J S Elliott

OUR PRINCESS DIANA

A great life has been taken from us
The short time we shared with Diana
Reading each day what the papers said
The young and old each shared her love
The way Diana reached out to shake their hands
Which brought warmth to their land
No matter what they were, black or white
Babies, youngsters and the very old
A smile said everything to them
Being there gave them so much trust
Wherever the journey was taking Diana
Across the far off shores
Her welcome was unforgettable
Just to see their faces
When Diana reached out her arms
And hugged the little ones
The look on their little faces
        Just said it all
        No need for words
        Just a smile from
        Our English Rose
          Diana

Ivy Blades

FULL STOP

Sitting watching the sun spin round,
onlooking only as others' lives go by;
only to end up in a hole in the ground.

Yet, as we sit atop a horse on a merry go round -
So many mysteries still to be found.
We try to listen but hear no sound.

The lottery numbers are picked for us;
One chance is the only one you'll get.
Wisdom, one finds, is only in Jesus:
We are all his fish. Will we end up in his net?

Now, as ever, we dance and fly -
Like children we dance and play.
But when the bell tolls, hear us cry.

How can we enjoy? How can we live?
Live a life that's full and try to give.
Don't run before you can crawl -
If this is followed, then life is a ball!
But what of identity? What about fun?
That's just Russian roulette with a shotgun.

Now, as ever, we dance and fly -
Trying always to be the brightest in the sky;
But there's no guarantee: we can only try.

If a sail is blown by two winds,
Will it not rip?
And if we are of two minds,
Have a nice trip.
Life gets you down, one finds,
And from death's icy glass we sip.

Stephan Wegner

REFLECTIONS

Sometimes I sit and wonder
How did I get here
My days are fraught with tension
My nights are filled with fear

When I first came to live here
I thanked my lucky stars
But my happiness did not last long
Now it's kept behind locked doors

This neighbourhood is violent
The people live for crime
I have to get away from here
It just might take some time

Nobody seems to care
About this fearful place
When I tell them where I live
I see pity on their face

So if you sit and wonder
Where it is I'm from
Take a look at your own back yard
And ask yourself 'How long'

A J De-Arden

LOVE STORY

Grey head on the pillow,
Eyes closed in deepest sleep,
Care lines round your features
Where time has written deep.
Grey head on the pillow,
You were so handsome, tall,
And of a crowd of fellows
Most charming of them all.
Grey head on the pillow,
To me you are the same,
A gentleman, desirable
As when I took your name,
Strange, now worn and weathered,
Old man! Your friends recall,
Like this I find I love you,
I love you most of all.

Vera Fertash

GRAPES ON THE VINE

High up in the Tuscan hills,
secluded from the northern chills,
luscious grapes grow on the vine
fruit that yields a heavenly wine.

Throughout the summer's heady days,
amidst the heat and dusty haze,
the vineyard master keeps a gaze
and tends the vines in this crucial phase.

From the oldest root to the newly crossed,
guarded from the midnight frost,
this precious fruit cannot be lost,
it must reach full ripeness at any cost.

Summer days have come and gone,
September's autumn rolls on and on,
the grapes are ready, and now's the time
to harvest them and make the wine.

Tread the grapes that make our wine
precious gift from sacred vine
making way, for in a year's time,
we'll have new grapes upon the vine.

Maria Gallo

LOCKED INSIDE

People I look up to
Because they're taller than me
I never look down on anyone
I'm no better than them you'll see
I am writing this down slowly
As I cannot read very fast
I have trouble communicating with people
They treat me as an outcast
If a person spits upon me
I swallow it with pride
Names they call me sometimes
I laugh them off but have never cried
When somebody threatens me
I just turn the other cheek
I am very strong inside
Never show I'm weak
Enemies I might have
But I love them every one
No one can hurt my feelings
No matter what they have done
I was born handicapped
I'm different from the rest
But to my father and mother
I'm more special and the best
If only I could speak my inner thoughts
I would tell them they are unique too
So precious loving thoughtful and kind
And I really do love you.

Jan Nice

I Love Scotland

I love Scotland isle like a jewel,
Heather covered mountains,
Air so clear and cool,
Pine clad mountains covered in winter snow
Tower over hungry deer that graze in herbs below.
I love Scotland, land of my birth,
The plaintive cry of seagulls that wheel over Solway Firth.
I love pipers whose tunes ring loud and clear,
Sunsets over Arran are things that I hold dear,
Oh yes, I love Scotland, Scotland the brave.

Helen Manson

TO FORGIVE IS DIVINE

To err is human, to forgive divine.
How often must I quote you that old line?
Anyone would think it was my intention
to leave you standing at the station.
I forgot the time!

I bought you flowers to cover my blunder.
You sneezed so much it made me wonder
how many people have hay fever in winter.
To err is human.

I booked a holiday, sea, sand and sunshine,
but your reaction made me whine.
How was I to know that you burn so easily,
your eyes swell up and your chest gets wheezy?
I've said I'm sorry so will you throw me a line?
To forgive is divine.

Kathryn Morgan

PICTURES FROM WORDS

The artist stands with brush in hand, beside the restless sea,
I watch with awe, the strokes he paints, so flowing and so free.
The canvas once a pure white block, becomes a harbour scene,
And as the boats move to and fro, they're repeated on the screen.

This man with skill creates a work, so vibrant, full of life,
And I can feel and hear the sounds, of the harbour's joy and strife.
A young man bends to tend his nets, he's captured in that pose,
And an old man sleeping in the sun, will be always in repose.

Perhaps I lack this artist's skill, but somewhere I have found,
A smaller gift, just mine alone, the love of words and sound.
And as the artist, I can paint, the pictures from my soul,
But the oils I use, are the words I write, as I print them on a scroll.

I write about the things I love, the people and their lives,
The funny things, the pleasant things, my emotions to survive.
And as the artist paints his scenes, a record for all to see,
I type my scenes in black and white, for all eternity.

I turn the pages one by one, and transpose the day and time,
And I can feel and see again, the moments and the clime.
The heat of day, the chill of night, the stars, the sun, the moon,
A special scene, the words we spoke, in the morning or at noon

A great despair, a haunted look, an emotion deep and bare,
A helpful word, a gentle look, and you are there to care.
A happy moment, full of fun, great laughter, shared by all,
The time we cried, a princess died, each second to recall.

So artist paint, in colours bright, hang your landscapes on the wall,
One picture's worth a thousand words to make you walk so tall.
But if I write one thousand words, ten thousand scenes I'll see,
And we can see them all again, if they're recorded so by me.

Janet Allen

MY LIFE

A life so busy,
And yet so empty.
A life of yearning,
For something unknown.
A life unsatisfied,
An unquenchable thirst.
A life of uncertainty,
Afraid and alone.
A life of ambition,
Hard work and strife.
A life but forgotten,
What kind of a life?

Claire Haughin

HA! HA! HA!
(To the stud who lightened up my life!)

Saturday morning 1 a m
Your doorbell goes once more.
You know he's been out with his mates,
And turned up at your door
Why can't he just phone you
At a decent hour of day?
Oh, that's too much like commitment,
And of course, that's not his way!
He expects to stay for breakfast.
And spend next day with you.
You just can't make arrangements
What he wants, you'll have to do!
After four years of this treatment
Why can't he see it in your eyes
That you're getting so fed up with him?
Why can't he realise
That you need a Christmas card
And a birthday card as well?
You really can't take much more of this
You wish he'd go to hell . . .
But then you meet the local stud
And invite him to your flat
And while you're having fun inside
Leave him outside on your mat!

Lynn Harper

THE ROAD OF LIFE

I have always loved you
From the very start
You are the one that made me
In my mind and in my heart

The road of life came in phases
It changed from day to day
But when the road was daunting
You were there to show the way

I thought I knew the answers
The world I would ignite
But when the road came darker
You were the one that gave me light

The road has many turnings
It was hard to keep on course
But like a river keeps on flowing
You became my source

Now I'm older and more wiser
Like a book that's just been read
But my heart is deep in sorrow
At words I never said

Father you are gone now
Your place I'll never fill
Though the road is now clearer
Goodbye makes the journey harder still

Terry White

THE SILENCE OF THE NIGHT

In the silence of the night
Thoughts emerge in the exhausted mind
Memories are retrieved
And those of sadness are the outcome

In the silence of the night
Alone in one's own surroundings
Tears flow
Expressing the pain of one's soul

In the silence of the night
Reluctance fades whilst memories arise
And the mind is overflowed
With events of the past

In the silence of the night
The exhausted mind yearns to rest
In the hope of forgetting and postponing thoughts
Impossibility arises

The mind continues emerging thoughts
Influential events holding the vital key to one's sadness
Hours yet to come and the mind's thoughts await
In the silence of the night

Nathalie El-Korashy

PRAYER

Father my heart is troubled,
How heavy seems my load.
Lord help me not to falter,
Uplift me and uphold.
Throughout my heart torn trouble,
Please send the sun to shine,
Oh! may my load be lifted,
Thy loving hand devine.
Before my stumbling footsteps,
Thy guiding star to lead.
Within my soul inward peace,
Thy love supply my need.

Vera Porter

VAMPIRE

In my world I live in,
I only see night
I fly through the skies
The stars are my light
I've flown across continents
And oceans vast
My eyes have witnessed, centuries past.
I will find you one day
It is meant to be
My love, my desire, my destiny
You will come to me
Without hesitance or fear
My world is a better one
Than you have here
I will dissolve your tears
That mortals give
You will have my heart
And forever live
Enfolded in my arms
Where you would gently sleep
And you would have, my soul to keep.

Caz Rioche

THE CHILD

I remember living
in the loneliness of a Cumbrian valley,
remote, lost in the hills,
the farm a white shadow
cast on the towering mountains,
lost in the silence of the echoing rivers,
in the green woods where the sun
crossed the bracken,
and the bluebells grew unseen, wild,
like the child watching.
I miss the long stretching summer days
the stream sliding over stone,
but I only have to close my eyes
to see the child,
only listen with my soul
to hear her.

Catherine Whittaker

It's Only a Game

Two little boys in a game of dreams and imaginations,
Mega swords, and light years,
Losing his balance in a warp,
With a *Ca-pow!* And *zap!*
Back into time,
Back to life.
Only a stick in his hand a token of something alien,
Cries of injury and pain,
Words of delight, 'It's only a game.'
Descriptions - helmets, spacesuits, visors all shining,
Karate chops and staggering back lying on the grass.
Hands up . . . power up,
The next line planned, then practised, acted out.
Dragons, purple people, spaceships and rays,
Power! Power!
Black to green, blue to red,
Lying dead.

Back to life . . . A game.

Aline McInnes Ross

THE MIDNIGHT STALLION

A movement in the shadows a sound upon the night,
the midnight stallion stands up tall,
his eyes all wide and bright.

With head held back, his nostrils flare,
to catch the scent upon the air,
he's master of the land around the leader of the night,
the midnight stallion will not back down,
he will always stand and fight.

A nervous feeling through the herd,
a sound, a smell, the movement of a nearby bird,
and sound of water in the brook, the stallion rears
to take a look.

For men will come with rope and gun,
his family they take one by one,
foal and filly young and old,
but midnight stands so proud and bold.

He fights them all to save his kin,
but he knows he'll never win,
for men are men,
and he's but horse,
and they have guns, a powerful force.

Shaun Gilbertson

SOMEONE SPECIAL

She would toddle along, with a pram full of dolls,
Everyone of them neat as a pin,
'You mustn't get cold - it's a nasty old day'
She would whisper, whilst tucking them in.
She was always the same - such a dear little soul,
I have known her since she was a tot,
When her brother was born, she would stay by his side,
And sing him to sleep, in his cot.
They grew up together, 'twas lovely to see.
Then one day I looked - and I saw there were three!
She never complained at the muddle they made,
And would hurry to tidy it up . . .
She is just the same now, when she brings me my tea,
(Taking care of my very best cup)
All the shopping gets done, and there's never a fuss,
When the queue is so long that she misses the bus,
She is just like a daughter, is my little Sarah.
I can never repay what I owe to my carer.

Brenda Baker

My Lady

I have loved my lady since first I saw her there,
I did not know from whence she came nor did I even care.
With eyes as dark as blackest night she stole my heart that day,
I knew then I could not leave without her, dare I say?
She came to me and standing close, her scent it was divine,
I knew I had to have her, had to make her mine,
Her hair was like the finest silk that China could supply,
To leave her would have torn my heart and made the angels cry,
I vowed to take her home with me, my feelings would not hide,
She returned with me, it's true, forever by my side,
She won my heart that day, I know, now she belongs to me,
She loves me, as I do her, it's plain for all to see,
Her face it is the noblest one that I have ever seen,
She is my lovely darling one, my sweetheart and my queen,
Who is this vision, this woman who has made me really care?
Why, can't you see she's Lady, my beautiful nut-brown mare?

Frank Richards

MILLENNIUM RESOLUTIONS

Dreams fade
Ambitions cease
Mediocrity, a friend.
Fires, only embers
Does anyone mind.
Millennium creeps nearer
challenging those
busy going nowhere.
It's the carrot
of no-hopers
tempting change
fuelling dreams.
Well at least
a New Year's resolution.

Carolyn Coyne

SLEEPY DARTMOOR

How low the clouds seem today
Drifting, skimming the sombre hills.
The earth lethargic after hibernal rest,
Jealously, it clings to slumber still.

Bright, golden gorse, fully awake,
Shines as a beacon midst near-dead growth,
The landscape, still desolate in this early spring,
Reluctant to shake off winter's sloth.

The blackened tors rise gaunt and stark,
Wrapped in low mist as if in death's shroud,
The awakening will be gradual and slow,
Before the moor is hospitable to summer crowds.

Just as the Creator Himself rose from Calvary's tomb,
His earthly miracle will soon arise,
Life will return to this slumbering place
And spring will unfold its beauty to our eyes.

Then the sun will tease out verdant spikes of green,
Heather will plump out its grains of purplish-blue,
Heat haze will hang over the distant tors,
Resplendent, Dartmoor will bask in its summer hues.

Pat Heppel

CLASSIC GOLD WE LOVE YOU

Classic gold we love
You
So the listeners
Shall never feel
Blue
And broadcasts all
Over the English
Nation
To a new and past
Generation
In the north,
South, east and
West
For Classic Gold
Is better than
All the
Rest
And is simply the
Best
With lots of famous
Guests

Coleen Bradshaw

FOREVER (LIFE MUST GO ON)

Spring - each year brings with it,
Thoughts of birth - and young, born a-new,
While to others - old-age appears,
And becomes part of the view.

Growth in its own - prepares,
For its next move to make,
To give some - a new beginning in life,
While to others - the hand of goodbye to wave.

Once silent shoots - speak,
- As they burst forth -
And say a final farewell to those,
For whom- no return ticket has been bought.

- Life in the making -
Guided by mother nature's hand
With no need of a classroom or alphabet,
To learn of what the future has planned.

Together - 'The creator' and 'The producer.'
Of the greatest show on earth,
In which beauty has been shared
By the eyes of the beholder,
Ever since the day - she first gave birth.

Bakewell Burt

THROUGH A GLASS, BRIGHTLY

My short-sighted sisters of spectacle and frame,
Wearers of the round, tinted, and the square:
Your sight may be poor, but I love you just the same.

For I remember well when first to the optician's I came:
As a small boy, I was afraid, but I found that they care.
Seeing the world through my glasses was a whole new game.

So to mock someone of limited visual fame
Shows lack of insight, and is most unfair:
We were made imperfect, and should not take the blame.

Should I remove my specs, a normal appearance my aim,
I find only bizarre impressionist blurs, as I squint and stare.
Once I tried contact lenses, but they my orbs did inflame.

Image is a hard thing to preserve without maim,
But these days you can buy a trendy pair:
Varied styles, modern or traditional, to light fashion's flame.

In fact, as an intellectual you can make a name
Communicating a businesslike air.
Sitting in the corner reading 'The Times' you can claim
To read the small print, an excuse far from lame.

David Tallach

GARDEN OF EDEN

When love takes root
Flowers grow
Giving birth to glory
Don't plant hatred
It kills the shoot
Destroying the colours of love

The soil is fertile
The soil is good
Bringing forth good things
But if left uncared for
Bad deeds take fruit
Killing the flowers of love

So keep on tilling
The soil of love
And plant in it good seed
Avoid pollutants
They add to harm
The innermost depths of need

A weakened soil
Takes anything
Whether it be good or bad things
It's at that moment
God works his deed
To save the soil from sin

So give it life
Give it truth
Give it what it craves for
A blessed harvest of all things good
Just treat the soil with love

Lea Rochelle

Today

Yesterday was a bad day,
it rained all day.
Only one room in the house was warm.
I had a bath,
when I finished I was still, cold and dirty.
I went to bed,
but it was damp and smelt funny.

Today is a strange day,
I got up,
from a perfumed warm bed.
I had a shower,
and now I'm clean and dry.
But I'm in a,
different house and I don't know where I am.

J Palmer

YOUR PICTURE

I still have your picture up on the wall
I look at it until I fall
Asleep at night
I often find I am talking to you
There's no answer, I know that's true
It doesn't seem right

If only your picture would answer me
We'd speak of old times, how it used to be
Those days are past
Then I let my mind run wild
Always dreaming like a child
'Till I'm asleep at last

If only your picture would come alive
It would help me to survive
This loneliness
Imagination I know runs wild
It helps me to be reconciled
With happiness

But should your picture materialise
And come alive before my eyes
How would I feel
Would feelings of love cause great strain
Would I return to sadness again
The hurt won't heal

So, I still have your picture on the wall
I still look at it until I fall
Asleep at night
Perhaps I imagine I'm talking to you
You're in my mind I know that's true
But out of sight.

Keith Farley

FOR THE LOVE OF ONE SON - GENTLE GIANT

A heart as big as a mountain
A body as tall as a tree
A temper as fiery as a volcano
His humour, witty as can be

Hands that are large but tender
Eyes that shine like an evening sea
Honest and caring his nature
Jolly and yet hopeful is he

Complex and cantankerous he can be
To stand tall and proud as a man
To love and be loved are his wishes
Peter my kind gentle man

Susan Goldsmith

FEELING SAFE

I often think of the people without any faith at all.
I couldn't survive a single day without my dear Lord to call.
The prayers I say I know he hears, he is there whenever I'm sad
He listens and always picks me up, that surely makes me glad.
Most of my friends are church friends but some of them are not,
The faith that I have I would gladly share, as I have enough to spare.
It's strange because the answer is in his sacrifice to save
His love and guidance forever
His life he gladly gave.

Jean Calver

THOSE LAZY DAYS OF SUMMER

I like to sit and think back to when I as very small
When all the gown-ups looked so big and all the trees so tall.

When laughter stayed around a lot and troubles they were few
Those lazy summer days we had, with nothing much to do.

We'd walk along the country lanes we didn't have a care
We could feel the grass beneath our feet, there was magic in the air.

We'd lay on the embankment and watch the trains go by
The clouds of smoke from the engine would swirl into the sky.

The buttercups looked so yellow, the grass it looked so green
The apple blossom the prettiest that I have ever seen.

A scene straight from a storybook is what I remember most
If I had died and gone to heaven I'd never be that close.

The sun it always seemed to shine even through the rain
The birds they sang the sweetest songs, as we walked back home again.

A lovely coloured butterfly would suddenly catch my eye
The smell of the wild flowers in the hedge as we walked by.

I was aware of many things when I was very small
But those lazy days of summer I loved the best of all.

Violet Bainbridge

FOREVER HOPEFUL

I am forever hopeful of the times we'll spend together -
Golden hours that we will turn into -
Golden days
Golden nights
Golden years
I am forever hopeful

At night I hear you singing
Of love and hope and joy
I want to draw you near
As if you were my little boy
I am forever hopeful

In times of fear and sadness
And each time you shed a tear
I want to soothe and comfort you
And show you that I care
I need to give you all my love
And stop this silent suffering
I am forever hopeful

I am forever hopeful
That you will see the light
And banish all the darkness
Let us be shining lights
I am forever hopeful

We can't go on forever without changing
Not our love
Not our relationship -
But our surroundings
I am forever hopeful

Why don't you see the joy you're missing
And come home to me at once
So that I can wrap my arms
Around my treasured gifted prince
I need to give my love to you
As much as I can give
And stop this silent suffering
Before it is too late.
I am forever hopeful.

Mia Ryan

FUTURE

God's creations great and small,
Should be preserved and free to all,
But man, with instincts of a killer,
Ruins these gifts with sprays and tiller.

Not 'til we've ruined each precious gift,
Will the mass opinion shift,
To try and save what has been free,
The land, the sky, a leaf, the sea.

What we do now, in years to come,
Will leave a legacy of scum,
Areas where one cannot tread,
Or like the planet we will be dead.

Golden sands and leafy paths,
You will only see on photographs,
But tread not there in years to come,
For you, my child, will walk in scum.

R A Sangster

Cosy

Warm scattered light's oh so cosy,
I wish I was in there.
Warming aura's pink and rosy,
Without them, the hills would be bare.

Windswept tree's nearly bending over,
Chimneys puff out smoke.
In awe I was made quite sober,
This vision is no joke.

Birds now resting, becoming dark,
The moon puts in an appearance,
The lamenting singing of the lark,
Hoping for no interference.

Cosy, cosy, warm and dry,
The lights they keep on calling.
No matter how much I try,
My senses they keep mauling.

Sleeping hillside, sleepy and content,
Really makes me feel it's heaven-sent.
For its beauty I could fall,
I know this was truly meant.

Gail Susan Halstead

My Day At The Races

The turf was lush, a lovely green,
The stands were full, from beam to beam,

Every face could tell a tale,
as they stood with lenses at the running rail.
Some with money to throw away,
and some with just a pound each-way.

Horses, trainers, owners too
stand and chat the first race through.
Jockeys with their coloured silks, look so tiny
as if in need of stilts.

Then at last the parade is ending,
so it's to the start, their judgement pending.
The bets are laid, the books are closed
the winners? No one knows.

The crowd go wild, one mighty cheer
as the winning-post draws near.
Then like a flash they're past the post,
the happy punters drink a toast.

Racing is over, we all depart.
the racecourse is empty, a ghostly quiet.
Horses and trainers go back to base,
to train again for another race.

So once more again, it's work, rest and play
that's why I love horse racing,
It makes my day!

D W Andrews

DONALD'S DAY

Your 18th birthday has come around
Today you are a man
Live your life to the full
Enjoy it while you can
Getting old ain't much cop
Just fill your life with fun
The next milestone that you reach
you will be twenty-one
It's when you get to thirty
and your hair it thins and goes
and you've got a pair of spectacles
sitting on your nose
Then when forty comes along
the booze it brings you down
Your belly starts a sagging
and it drags along the ground
But when you get to fifty
your bones begin to creak
and all the parts that were working
give up and fall asleep
So Donald enjoy your special day
A great future lies at your door
Be grateful for small mercies
Be happy ever more.

Sylvia E Armer

Win Some, Lose Some

Life is a game of tiddlywinks,
Whether you want to play or not:
You can have the fun and high jinks,
But it's hard to hit the pot!

You line the tiddlies in a row,
All ready for the sport,
And one by one you let them go,
But most of them fall short,

Or fly into the air and land
Far from their destination;
Our steady aims and careful plans
End often in frustration.

An onlooker would never guess,
By looking at the tiddle,
That a course so devious
Was aimed towards the middle.

But now and then we have a spot
Of unexpected luck!
Two tiddlies in succession drop
Straight down into the cup!

But then there are the squoppers
Who, by accident or design,
Flip their winks onto others'
And make them bide their time.

They can go on squidging
Whilst others watch and wait;
It's really very trying
- A tiddlywinker's fate.

Yes, life is a game of tiddlywinks:
It falls unto our lot
To have the fun and high jinks,
But it's hard to hit the pot!

Doreen Priestley

ON THE BEACH

Putting this shell to your ear
You will hear old sea songs,
Taste the salt
And feel the heaving deck,
See the wing-long albatross
And dolphin's play.

A quiet lagoon
Lapping a tropic shore
Mirror for the Southern Cross
A thousand miles away.

While you are there
Allow a thought or two
To steal away
To where I lie
Watching these sliding streams
Through half closed eyes,
Cold avalanches
In the sands of home.

A P Dixon

DISUSED AIRFIELD

Here cattle crop the grass and straggling weeds have grown
Between some granite blocks of broken stone
And there a hanger derelict
From weather and neglect
Is falling down.
The runway just a rough brown
Line across this open space
An ever poignant sign
That here in this deserted place
Heroic deeds were done.
And in the sighing wind - hear
A spitfire's engine roar
And see those youthful ghosts appear
Returning to the scene from where
They fought their final war.
Those days of darkness long since gone
Memories fade and life moves on.
The council has already planned
A building project on this land
Fifty houses and a school
A bingo hall and swimming pool
Machinery is moving in
Soon excavations will begin
Sewage pipes well concealed - electric cable laid
Upon this weed infested field
Where history was made.

Jessica Frank

A Writer's Commission

All I have done goes into the sands of time,
It is only the words I write that live on in people's hearts,
And go on as a testimony of my life work,
All I have ever written back to dust will go
but words live on and impart wisdom,
Which means more to me than a hundred books,
If through my words I can impart faith, hope and love
I have not failed but succeeded!

Julie McKenzie

True Friend

A friend is someone you value
When your family leaves home to get wed
When the chores of the day are over
The thoughts that come into your head

The happiness you have shared together
Is something you never forget
It lingers forever in your memory
As you wish them all the best

A friend is of the greatest value
When you begin to be depressed
This is when you realise the true friend
You will value to the very end

Edna Ball

FINAL JOURNEY OF A PASSENGER LINER

Slowly she left the sunny shores and moved out to the ocean
Left behind the bargainers and much dockside commotion
Steaming homeward, full of mail and final passengers aboard
Echoes sound across the water as the sad watchers applaud.

Young officers in gleaming whites weigh up the female talent
Planning amorous homeward nights, while appearing gallant.
Down below, the pistons throbbing, men at work in noise and heat
Engineers and greasers bobbing, noting every pulsing beat.

Decks once trod by Freetown sailors singing as they scrubbed the poop
Men with names like Smith and Taylor, Willie Turner and Pea Soup!
Waiters with a ribald jest strive to make the bar cards tally
Steward types the manifest while Cookie labours in the galley.

Passing Finnisterre, the Lizard, docks, then passengers departed
Final journey starts in blizzard. Skeleton crew are heavy hearted
Ploughing thru the icy waters north from Tilbury to Leith.
Going like a lamb to slaughter, no-one there to throw a wreath.

Echoes of her past still clinging in the cabins cold and bare
Sounds of crewmen's band and singing in the bulkheads everywhere
Clocks removed from wood partitions,
                                      lights unscrewed from each saloon.
Ship, once sleek, in poor condition. Alleyways with rubbish strewn.

At the breakers' yard she's tied next to other ships half flayed.
Crew and baggage all gone shore side. She awaits the cannonade.
Some there were who mourned her ending. Secretly keepsakes acquired
In their homes you'll find them tending items
                                      saved when she was fired.

Diana Griffiths

OUTSIDE OF BASINGSTOKE

We went for a walk,
'Twas a lovely spring morn.
We passed by some fields
Of lovely green corn.

The air was so fresh
As we climbed up the downs.
We could see for miles
As we left the town.

And there in the meadow
Was a sheep with two lambs.
They were born last night
And could hardly stand.

And farther on there was another
She had two black lambs.
Though she was all white
She was their true mother.

Further on were some primroses,
And a few cowslips too.
Just a few daises and violets
In the grass peeping through.

We finished our walk.
It was nice to sit down.
A meal cooked by one man,
For twenty-two of us - without a frown.

Margaret E Gaines

LISTEN TO US OUR RIGHTS

Oh why is it governments never list to us?
They are taking us into Europe, we shouldn't make a fuss
But I was born in a free happy country which I don't want to lose
I know which people like me if had rights would choose
EC would rise taxes we couldn't afford to pay
And our interest rates are rising now the very same way
We were promised a referendum, can't see it can you?
You may think it does not matter try to stop it coming true
Freedom of speech we've always had over here
But now the price of our freedom seems very dear
We deserve the freedom we've always had
Things in our country today go from good to bad.

Velma Winstanley

STILLNESS

And I said unto myself, inside, be still,
For in the calmness of mind,
A wind shall blow,
And rain clouds shall gather,
Fine beyond the horizon,
Whose fluttering flag is calleth understanding.

And in its silent wake,
A stranger called Peace,
Drew near the open fire,
That warmeth the many roomed house,
And said unto the flames,
'How bright thee flicker in the dark,
Whose shadows fall ill to resist,
The music of your love.'

And in response,
Such luminous dancers,
Threw open their heart,
In the joy of untainted release,
And wept a song of shameless praise.

No words escaped their burning lips,
To rise as thieves,
To steal the sun,
Who ripens the fruit,
In splendid groves of ancient repute,
Whose only intention is love,
As they murmur unto themselves.

Dave Mountjoy

NEON ANGELS

Many times they walked the coast road
to lay upon the shingle shore,
the cover of darkness hid
their mid-summer madness.

The sky alive at night
Aurora borealis, pink and blue
fantailed across blood-orange sea.
We have our beginnings here.

Of honeysuckle and lilac time they loved
faces mirroring each other's love
and slept in bay-lulled calm
while gentle lapping tapped the shore.

A scattering of shore birds pecked limpets
down to the rolling expanse of the sea
dragonflies darted like neon angels
as silver spectres up to Siren fly.

The seeming insignificance's of stars
proclaimed these wondrous happenings
like something gathering in spate
all that summer long.

Until the birch leaves
cut that day, had closed and withered
as if with the heat of their loving
or the ravenings of unfilled hunger.

Carole House

LIFE CAN BE SWEET

Today I smell the sweetness of life
I was once a confident, lover and wife
No more. I hide away or act the fool
Gone are my shackles and my brick wall.

If I can wake up with a smile on my face
Then it can't be bad to be part of the human race
Positive energies surround my world
Me, slowly but surely, I'm starting to uncurl.

I feel, at last, I've a right to be
Kindred spirits around me, all help me to see
This journey of mine won't be without its strife
Today I smell the sweetness of life.

P A Deakin

A Career In IT

I never imagined I would be
A pioneer woman in IT.
I had no desire to maintain
Close relationship with computer screen.

I had thought I would see
Patients in a surgery,
Who would place their faith in me,
To ease their aches and pain.
I imagined.

Suffering as a minority,
A focus of male repartee.
Hours of silence would be a strain,
The technical would hurt my brain.
IT could never make me happy,
I imagined.

Suzanne Fowler

AUGUST '96

For as many
the truth you found
that which went up
had to come down
and within those brown eyes
I saw
that pain and sorrow had found a home once more.

Yes, you had known pain
had known so much
I realised in one single touch
I looked again
and you were strong
at least enough to carry on.

We talked awhile
shared a drink
had time enough to remember and think
of past times good
and past times bad
remembering the happy and the sad.

Then all at once
was time to go
where to, I will never know
I turned around
and she was gone
our lives now separate
for we had moved on!

Samuel Down

GOD'S RAINBOW

There is hope at the end of God's rainbow,
There is love at the heart of His plan,
There is trust that His love will uphold us
Each child, each woman, each man.
There is always a hand to guide us,
There is always a listening ear,
There is always an understanding heart
When God is near.

His love is everlasting,
His comforting hand always near,
His spirit is all around us,
To guide, to love, and to cheer,
God's rainbow was His promise
That the world should know His love.
And always find a resting place,
In His heavenly home above.

Barbara Quimby

I Saw A Butterfly

I saw a butterfly today,
a chosen moment
on the twelfth of the twelfth.

My eyes struggled to
follow its flight,
small and delicate
fluttering between winter
twigs and debris.
Again I see it - colour bright,
sharing these seconds
with a life so short
is a truly wondrous thing.

Karen Monaghan

MEMORIES

The house where I grew up till four
   is now no more.
Its creepy cellars candlelit,
the harness room with stabled horse,
the pigsty and the laying hens,
the wheel-less horse drawn bus on lawn,
the sash held shutters gainst the thief,
the outdoor privies still in use,
all missed the might of Hitler's war
   are now no more.
The next we lived in till the war
   is now no more.
Where babbling brook and fields of corn,
and skyline trees, where rising sun
bade me set off for city's gloom:
the school which taught me read and write
and listened to my schoolboy verse,
from which I gained a grammar place:
the house where first I hugged by bride,
where countless Me's were locked inside
   they are no more.
My teacher's college stood the war
   but is no more.
The spaces sandbagged gainst the bomb,
the forty winks, the siren's wail -
up all night long then out to school:
a quick goodbye then off to war -
how memories come flooding back:
   the places are no more.
The thousand children I have taught
their sums and writing, faith and love,
these memories they hold in store
   for now and ever more.

Owen Edwards

TRUSTING PEOPLE

Trusting people
Is part of life
Just as learning
Wrong from right
Betraying a friend
Loosing the trust
Breaking up is a must
Sharing secrets
There is no more
Just an empty feeling
And your heart is sore
You loose the faith
As you lost a friend
It feels like the world will end
Bear with it
And you'll get through
There's nothing on earth
That you can't do.

Danielle Turner

The Alcoholic

I look at you, your sad old face,
I've observed your life, felt your disgrace.
Seen that bottle in your yellowed hand,
and you think I wouldn't understand.

I've heard your tales and I've borne your lies,
thought I once glimpsed sincerity in those glazed old eyes.
I've picked you up when I've seen you fall,
I came running, if I heard you call.

But now's the time it all must stop,
you've drained this *bottle* of every drop.
I've stood before you, I've seen your rage,
but now it's time to act your age.

Stop this denial for we all can see,
you are an alcoholic, you no longer are free.
You're in a hole, can't find a way out,
and I think you forgot what life's all about.

Hitting the bottle may dull your pain,
until in sobriety it all comes again.
You must face the day with hope from within,
not in a stupor of whisky and gin.

I know you won't like this, see me as unfair,
but I want to help you, you see, I still care.
But if you don't get help, I'm sorry to say,
I'm walking away, there's no reason to stay.

Claire Partridge

Dream Children

In youth my dreams were for three
As though one picked them from a tree
Two boys . . . one girl . . . I thought ideal
But dreams, alas, are not real.

My blessing was a cherished daughter
All money on earth could not have bought her
The longed for sons eluded me . . .
then hope, but it was not to be.

So she was my son when we kicked a ball
But my little girl after a fall
Years of joy as mother and daughter
Then one day love came to court her.

So now my dreams are almost true
My children have grown from one to two
From my daughter although in-law
A loving son I now adore.

P McNeil

THE COPPERED DREAM

Slide into the coppered dream
Where sun rays scorch the earth
Blister bathed solarity
Invoke a heatwave's mirth
Liberally baste yourself
With bottled creams and oil
Then marvel at your frazzled skin
The prize for which you'll toil
Melanomic escapades
We feel the sun's warm hands
Whilst coveting the coloured skins
Of those from distant lands.

Kim Montia

WALK WITH ME

The last drops of rain,
Fell like gentle reminders.

Looking up at the sky
The man left his shelter,
It was a huge chestnut tree
That glistened in the rain,
Westward,
Huge cracks in the broken clouds
Let through a large, violent sunset.
Straight ahead the sky was dark slate
Untouched by the fire that melted the sky.
Every blade of grass and tree
Dripped with rain
And the road he travelled on,
Shone like a river.
Holding the hand of his wife
He said, 'Walk with me.'

The last drops of rain,
Fell like gentle reminders.

Paul Willis

FOOTPRINTS IN THE SNOW

For three long years you went away
And took with you my heart
I longed for you each night and day
While we were far apart
Our letters were the only things
That you and I could share
Of all the pain that parting brings
Made constantly aware
I missed you in so many ways
Your voice, your touch, your smile
Yet in my heart I knew our love
Would transcend every mile
Your picture at my bedside stayed
So that each day I'd see
Your handsome face when I awoke
There smiling down at me
Then came the day I'd waited for
My heart was beating fast
For word had come to say that you
Were coming back at last
Soft fallen snow around me lay
Where other feet had tread
Whimsically I wished that they
Could have been yours instead
Then suddenly I realised
That they led to my door
And there you were waiting for me
Back home to stay once more
So many years have passed since then
And still our love is strong
Within our hearts still certain that
Together we belong

On looking back I reminisce
Recapturing the glow
The poignant moment when I saw
Your footprints in the snow

Patricia Whittle

REMEMBERING ME

When you are huddled,
turned, ball like, against the chill.
When you feel the need of warmth,
a body whose heat you could steal
remember me.

When your lips,
all dry and in need of pressure,
when the need for another pair is great.
Just close your eyes,
and remember me.

When your bed swallows you,
a desert of loneliness,
and when you long for an oasis.
Just stop, think of the drink I give,
and remember me.

When your arms ache,
you feel the void between them grow.
When your body cries out for someone to hold,
a body to squeeze and to be a provider of the same,
remember me.

When I die,
when I am cast into the ground.
Remember the day we met,
rejoice in the memory, light a candle,
and remember me.

Ivan J Peck

SHARE A FOREST

Share a forest, come with me, a joy so free.
Let us walk the spongy path slowly,
See tall silver Birch reflecting light, while
Sunbeams dance around bush and bracken.
Shadows from boughs falling to the ground,
Light and dark scattered all around,
Snapping twigs crack beneath our feet
Sounding there to disturb melodious birds,
They dart among shaded light from tree to tree.
We sense the watching eyes from grass to bush
Of creatures reflecting our trespass.
The little mole a tiny mite, stoats, weasels
And rabbits we wish not to fright and run
To burrows hidden from our sight.
The dew damp grass is so fresh and green,
I love to share the forest life - so clean.
High above squirrels climb in gay abandon;
Where wise owls hoot, just another to scare.
So why not walk along a forest path?
See a world of creatures wild and free,
Enjoy your country walk, just like me.

Des Lamb

ONE TO ONE HUNDRED

One single thought inside the babe begins,
To live a life of simple things,
Express its needs, love wills the best
And leaves all hardship to the rest.

This too begins in hope, each century,
And every new relationship clears the deck,
But inheritance steals in upon us from old,
And waxes pains, child begins to grow.

Independence, separativity, problems show,
In every generation motives warp
To dull intelligence, complicate the soul,
Deaf to consequences, heart-blind we go.

Enters each individual and every century too
Into the 'why me' syndrome
Capped by resentment, fears and worries sue the spirit,
Lost to truth, deceived by worldly powers
We seek solutions, wisdom's light, to return home;
As one.
One race, one nation, one family, one unique individual.

Middle-aged we are, the century is past its prime.
Repent and reflect on bygones
Adds a little consciousness to time.

Then old we are, as winter withdrawn.
Our hidden self already shaped by choices made
Reveals itself to eternity
No cheating life, no concealing acts from God;
We hold naked our own destiny!

Marion Elvera

Just Perfect

Quaint old cottage with thatch roof,
Horse shoe on the door.
To bring good luck to those inside,
Belong in days of yore.

Handmade rugs upon stone floor,
Fire in the grate.
Glowing coals warm the room
And so for tea we wait.

Home-made bread and scones for tea
With strawberry jam and cream.
Melts in your mouth with every bite,
Gran's baking is supreme.

Grandfather clock ticks in the hall,
Its chimes they fill the air.
Time for grandpa to relax,
In his favourite rocking chair.

A twisting stair, old latch door,
Feather bed you sink so deep.
In eiderdown and pillows plump,
These memories I keep.

E Jones

PESSIMIST AND OPTIMIST

A pessimist I'm told I'll be
For I look to the bad in all I see
When life is good
And running smooth
I will begin a sombre mood
I'll think of the worse
And make myself worry
A problem so small
Is doubled in a hurry
Sceptical and cynical
Is my second name
I wish I wouldn't play this game

I can't believe I have
All this doubt
The feeling inside is
I really want to shout
'An optimist is what I should be'!
But o' can you imagine me
Expecting the best of everything
A bright and hopeful
Future I'll sing
I wouldn't have thought
That was me
For an optimist I'll never be

Sonia Coneye

My Pledge Of Honour

An oldness of feeling summons up ancient understanding of wanting this new world to end and the old to being again. Connection with the earth, trees, wind, fire and rain gives me the strength of comfort to carry on the fight against the beast. Which would deny me freedom to have these things, as it does others. Who by their own willingness choose to give up and live in a void of non-understanding.

The beast nurtures them and they in return suckle willingly on the milk of ignorance, hate and prejudice, only to find out too late their folly.

I say, better to be ridiculed by them, or crucified and tortured by the minions of the beast; than give up my belief in the powers that be and always have.

I say, hear me now; True forces of goodness and light:

I willingly defy all and everything in your name.

Blessed be.

Simon King

A Mum

Anyone can be a mother,
But not everyone can be a mum.

A mum, caring, who loves you always.
A light that seems close at the end of a distant tunnel.
The smile upon her graceful face,
Full of tenderness and sincerity.

A joke can always be shared between you,
Or, the seriousness when needed, always understood.
A feeling of you both being one,
Like long ago.

A heart melting, when in their presence,
From a cold hard stone,
Needed for the outside world,
Always a distinct forgiveness between us.

A mum knows how you feel,
Even when the strongest of masks protect you.
A mum, who can help you forget any sadness,
With one warm, comforting hug.

When a mum places those enclosing arms around you,
Problems just disappear, like when you were a small child.
One smile can wash all your worries away,
From the tender face of hers.

Yes, anyone can be a mother,
But not everyone can be a mum.

Sian Sparks

DIGGING HOLES

Digging holes is honest, digging holes is fun.
Work with lots of fresh air and plenty of sun.
Have a drink after work, keep your spirits high
But never stop digging while life passes by.
Dig holes in your life, dig holes in your mind.
Keep on digging and like the moles you'll stay blind.

And while you dig, we'll dig too.
We'll dig away your life from you.
All lost in forms and timetables and post office queues.
Swapped for a giro or a case of the diggers' blues.
But keep on digging my friends, the hole never ends
Because we'll never stop you to make amends.

Dig six feet under, dig further still.
Keep on digging until you're over the hill.
And when you have dug and you lie on your death bed, remember your children who'll dig until they're dead.

John Dobson

TALES FROM THE RIVERBANK

Down by the riverbank, hours we've spent.
I tell you 'I love you', every word I have meant.
The animals have ears!

A fox takes a peak, so arrogantly and sly.
And there above the river, hovers an eavesdropping dragonfly.
A squirrel sits patiently on a branch of a tree,
While owl turns his head so he too can see.

Badger is prowling beneath the hedgerows quite near
And rabbit is listening with large pointed ears.
A frog at the river's edge reveals its hideout with a croak.
This is all now becoming a bit of a joke.

Then a magpie takes flight, he's heard enough,
As we whisper sweet nothings so deeply in love.
And as we leave back to our house,
You'd never believe it, *'squeak, squeak',* it's that mouse.

John Palmer

ANOTHER WORLD

They tremble through my home
Never bidding time of day
Those poor weak children
From a continent so far away.
Their eyes are large, in dust grained faces.
Tummies large, not from gorging
But from hunger blown.
The sandy earth around, simmering in the sun,
Offers no hope, nor food to be found
To aid their plight.

They thread the boards for our amusement.
I cry, knowing of their pain.
Even though I care I cannot be there.
Conscience money in a box
Will calm for now, rest cannot come.
Their eyes grow bigger
And bellies larger,
Until my mind explodes,
Not capable of coping
With this worry for another world.

Teresa Smith

WAITING

Toiled earth that holds
A thousand memories
Shielded by hedges bright with breath
Of morning light

Her season's are a moments thought
And my presence will be
As easily wiped away
But you remain
Waiting for the next hand
To score your face.

Patricia Wardle

TROUBLE

Consumed a fine meal, left one's wallet at home.
That's what most people would call 'slight trouble'.
Arriving at the church on the wedding day late,
Wrong church and wrong date! That's female trouble!
Drunk, demolished a squad car outside a police station.
Immediate irate response. That's sure trouble!
Defrauded many poor people out of millions of pounds,
To rest in the lap of luxury in far off grounds. Hardly trouble!
Hacked into a bank's computers and milked their accounts.
Shhhhh, they wanted it hushed up! That's no trouble at all!
Hustled stolen Visa cards, squandered massive amounts.
Inevitably others pay the price. Why, that's not trouble!
Drove madly around the town and ran some people down.
Failing to report an accident. That's impending trouble!
Got a life sentence for murder, reducing for good behaviour.
Languished, locked up in a luxury cell. Time consuming trouble!
Married a pretty wife with a tongue sharper than a Stanley knife.
That's pure, unadulterated, hundred per cent proof, real trouble!

T Burke

WHY WORRY

Love had found a reason why I was born.
My journey through life was mine, from then on.
I learnt to eat, then to talk,
Before I found that I could walk.
Now I have grown and found my way,
I intend to enjoy myself everyday.
Worries and troubles is a torment sown.
Life is too short to sit and moan.
Love and laughter is my way,
Before my youth fades away,
Leaving me a decrepit old man someday.
Life is a heaven on earth for me,
Until the crematorium disposes of me.
What may happen next I cannot tell,
Then they will have 'roasted me in hell . . .'

Brian Marshall

I Love You More Everyday

I love you more, much more everyday
knowing you are closer and not far away
The more I do love you, much more you do care
you're a part of my heart that is always there
You begin in my stories that never has an end
You'll always be my mother, also a friend
You're a story of my happiness and also a song
You're a chapter, a verse in my heart you belong

I love you more, much more everyday.
You're the wind in my hair that keeps me at bay
You're the night-time stars that sparkle so bright
You glimmer in my heart and dreams at night
You venture to meet me in some distant land
You guide me in my sleep, you are there to understand

Terry Collins

IF ONLY LIFE WAS A BALL OF WOOL

If only life was a ball of wool, then we could undo the things we have done.
Unpick the silver threads we put in mum's hair, to make her a shawl of comfort and care.
Take our impatience with people and places, to knit up a bright sweater of smiling faces.
All our uncertainty, ifs, buts or whats, could make a cosy warm pair of socks.
To undo all our mistakes would be very nice, but then we would do things without thinking twice.
Perhaps then it's better to look back on mistakes or loose ends, just to remind us we all have good friends.
These special people who accept us as we really are, still caring about us, even when we go too far.
Everyone knows it's impossible to be perfect just some of the time, but our friends don't judge our many crimes.
If we can apologise with feeling from our heart, then we can begin to make a fresh start.
When we are hurting our anger we can't hide, true friends can forgive us, as they see what's inside.
A friend or lover can see the pain felt inside, and will patiently wait for the storm to subside.
When it's all over and we're feeling ashamed, we know our indiscretions will never be named.

Veronica Black

APART NO MORE

Rise sleepy head waken for sure
Vision of innocence came to view
Pale complexion lit midnight room
Motionless lips whisper welcome words
Come forth is all was heard
Fall asleep at rest again
For many weeks encounter remained
Until one cold November night
A stranger not came into sight
Conversation in graceful tune
Rested smiles under full lit moon
Fate responded to abandon call, after all
Together again. Apart no more.

Alan Jones

I Am You

It's my eyes that stare back at you
Each time you touch her face
It's my skin you feel
In your warm embrace.
It's my perfume that lingers in the intimate
Moments that you share.
It's the picture of me in your mind, you know,
I'm always there.
For all eternity this feeling will always be.
I am part of your very soul my darling,
I am you, as you are me.

Tracy Mitchell